WILD CANINES!

WOLF

By Jalma Barrett
Photographs by Larry Allan

BLACKBIRCH PRESS, INC.

WOODBRIDGE, CONNECTICUT

Published by Blackbirch Press, Inc.
260 Amity Road
Woodbridge, CT 06525

Email: staff@blackbirch.com
Web site: www.blackbirch.com

©2000 by Blackbirch Press, Inc.
First Edition

Printed in the United States

10 9 8 7 6 5 4 3 2 1

All photographs ©Larry Allan.

Dedication
For Brian

–JB and LA

Library of Congress Cataloging-in-Publication Data
Barrett, Jalma.
Wolf / text by Jalma Barrett : photographs by Larry Allan.
     p.   cm. — (Wild canines!)
   Includes bibliographical references (p.) and index.
   Summary: Describes the physical characteristics, behavior, family life, hunting tactics, and life cycle of the animal with the distinctive howl.
   ISBN 1-56711-262-5 (lib. bdg.: alk. paper)
   1. Wolves—Juvenile literature. [1. Wolves.] I. Allan, Larry, ill. II. Title. III. Series: Barrett, Jalma. Wild canines!.
QL737.C22B3435   2000
599.773—dc21   99-32649
                                          CIP

Contents

Introduction

You spot a large, dog-like shadow keeping its distance from you as you walk through a northern forest or across an open tundra (flat, treeless arctic plain). If this forest phantom runs with its tail straight out behind it, you know you have seen a wolf. It might be called a gray wolf, timber wolf, tundra wolf, arctic wolf, or Mexican wolf, but they all belong to the same species—*Canis lupus*.

Large numbers of gray wolves once roamed North America, but many were killed by ranchers protecting their livestock. In the 1960s, gray wolves were close to extinction. Today, thanks to strict laws and protection, gray wolves live in many places.

Where Wolves Are Most Common

Wolf territory

Canada

United States

Mexico

Central America

4

They are found throughout Alaska and Canada, and in northern Washington, Montana, Minnesota, and Wisconsin. In 1995, they were re-introduced into Yellowstone National Park in Wyoming, and into parts of Idaho as well. Most recently, gray wolves were released in the Blue Mountains of southern Arizona.

Native Americans believe that wolves are great teachers. They respect the wolves' vast physical strength and endurance, as well as their unique ability to hunt and survive.

Gray wolves have come back from near extinction. Today they can be found in many parts of North America.

Physical Appearance

Wolves are large canids (dog-like animals). Their coats can range in color from black to white to gray and tan. They have long legs, and can weigh from 50 to 175 pounds (23–80 kilograms).

A gray wolf may be from 26 to 38 inches (66–76 centimeters) tall at the shoulder. A wolf's head and body measure 35 to 59 inches (90–150 centimeters) long. Their long bushy tails add another 14 to 20 inches (35–50 centimeters) to their length. Males are larger than females.

Arctic wolves range in color from white to cream.

One way to tell canines apart is by looking at their tails. Gray wolves run with their black-tipped tails straight out behind them. Coyotes are much smaller animals and carry their tails down. And dogs, descendents of wolf ancestors, carry their tails curved up.

Another way to recognize a wolf is by the shape of its face—its pointed ears and muzzle (nose and jaw) form a distinctive triangle. Its slanted yellow-gold eyes are outlined in black.

Gray wolves have thick coats and bushy tails.
Inset: Wolves can range in color from white to gray to black.

Special Features

One of the greatest survival skills that wolves possess is their endurance (long-lasting strength). To find food, wolves travel farther and more frequently than any other land-based mammal, except caribou. Wolves continuously move through pine woods, listening for sounds made by prey—sounds humans cannot hear. A wolf pack is able to hunt a territory of 100 to 260 square miles (260–675 square kilometers). An arctic wolf pack's territory is from 800 to 1,000 square miles (2,080–2,600 square kilometers) or more. With their distinctive loose-limbed trot, wolves cover their territory on a regular basis, usually along well-worn trails. They can cover 50 miles (80 kilometers) in 24 hours, day after day. Their excellent senses of smell and hearing help them track their prey.

Wolves' eyes, like those of other canines, face forward. This gives them the ability to accurately judge the distance of an animal they are stalking.

Top: Thick-furred paws help wolves run on top of the snow.
Below: Forward-facing eyes are best for judging distance and depth, especially while hunting.

Cries in the Night

Wolves are best known for their distinctive nighttime howls. While howling, a wolf lifts its head up at a 45-degree angle. This projects its voice straight ahead. Short barks from a member seem to start a pack howling. The barks are followed by long, low-pitched howls. Howling stimulates the wolves' urge to hunt. It also keeps the pack together when it is on the move. Generally, a wolf howls for no more than 5 seconds. Then another wolf will return the cry. Wolves usually howl individually. A howl might be at a constant pitch, or vary, rising and falling. Wolves also whine, growl, yelp, and bark.

Gray wolves communicate many things to other pack members through distinctive cries in the night. A wolf separated from the pack will give a specific lonesome howl—a short call that rises in pitch and fades to a plaintive sound. If the loner is answered, it will respond with what is called a location or assembly howl. This type of howl is deep and even, often punctuated by barks. Wolves stalking prey seldom call out. At the beginning of their chase, they do use sound to maintain contact with each other, or to signal they have reached a place of ambush. This sound helps other pack members locate the hiding place so they can try to chase their prey past that spot.

Howls are a complex form of wolf communication that can send many kinds of messages.

Social Life

Gray wolves live in extended family groups and pair off for life. This is called long-term pair bonding. Wolf groups live by strict rules of order. A pack includes a breeding pair and their offspring. Pups usually remain in the pack until they are about 3 years of age. The strongest wolf becomes the pack's leader, and is called the alpha. The alpha can be male or female. The alpha takes a mate, and the pair are usually the only ones in the pack that reproduce.

Baring teeth is one wolf sign of power and aggression.

Pack structure means every wolf has a designated place. For example, the alpha male and alpha female always eat first. Then the other wolves will eat in order of dominance (rank in the pack). Wolves show dominance over others by baring their teeth, raising the hair on their backs, pointing their ears forward, and holding their tails high. The higher the wolf holds its tail, the more authority it claims.

Wolves also show submission in many ways—they avert their eyes, lie on their backs, lay their ears back, or tuck their tails between their legs.

Subordinate wolves may go off on their own. Or, a wolf might be driven from the group after losing a battle for a higher place in the pack's structure. Because wolves are accustomed to surviving in packs, it is dangerous for a gray wolf to live on its own.

Wolf packs have a very strict social order. The alpha always leads and eats first. Laying ears back (inset) is one sign of submission.

The Pack Hunts

As the day ends, the pack gathers to hunt. The alpha wolf leads the way, and the pack follows as a unified team. The land on which they hunt may have been used by several generations of the pack. The territory is carefully marked with urine scent at intervals of about every quarter mile. The scent sends a message of ownership and warning to other wolves and can last up to 5 months. Both the alpha male and alpha female lift their leg to urinate. All other wolves—both the males and the females—squat.

Marking territory is an important part of wolf survival.

Wolves hunt by chasing down their prey. They will often use their sharp teeth to slash tendons in the prey's hind legs and knock it off its feet. Wolves can bring down an animal 10 times their own weight.

Even though wolves can run more than 30 miles (48 kilometers) an hour, a healthy deer can easily outrun them. A moose that fights back often convinces a wolf pack to look for easier game.

Wolves in a pack eat according to the social order. The alpha pair (leaders) always eat first.

Wolves also eat small animals—squirrels, rabbits, birds, and fish. They eat berries as well. The diet of an arctic wolf consists of arctic hares, musk ox, caribou, and lemmings (rat-like rodents). Mexican wolves hunt small deer, young elk, pronghorn antelope, and bighorn sheep. These animals can be taken down by a pair of Mexican wolves, rather than a large pack.

Mexican Wolf: Species Survival

During the 1970s, the Mexican gray wolf population reached an all-time low of about 50. In 1976, the U.S. government finally took action. It was then that Mexican wolves were protected under the Endangered Species Act. The last few wild wolves were captured in Mexico and Arizona and placed in captive (human-controlled) breeding programs for later release. Today, there are 39 places in

the United States and Mexico that breed Mexican gray wolves. These participants are part of the Species Survival Plan of the American Zoo and Aquarium Association. Through their work, they have raised the number of Mexican wolves to 130. Without the successful efforts of the participating facilities, zoologists could not have re-introduced 11 Mexican gray wolves into the southwestern United States in 1998.

Although wolves can fast (go without eating) for about 2 weeks, they generally need from 3.5 to 4 pounds (1.5– 2 kilograms) of meat daily. Wolves will gorge (eat greedily) when they do find food. They can eat up to 20 pounds (44 kilograms) of food in one meal. This over-eating helps them survive until they kill again.

Usually, animals that wolves attack are either sick, injured, or very young or old. Wolves will often test another animal's abilities to see if it can be killed easily. Gray wolves will surprise their prey by ambushing them. Wolves will

Wolves have the strength, energy, and hunting skills to track prey over long distances.

not chase their prey for long distances—they will only run about 1,000 yards before turning back. Sometimes they simply follow prey at a comfortable pace—for as long as 8 hours—until the hunted animal tires.

The Mating Game

Wolves reach maturity (the ability to reproduce) in their second year. In general, they don't mate until they are 3 years old. Mating takes place in February or March. Gestation (unborn development time) lasts for 63 days. Litter size varies from 1 to 12 pups, also called cubs. The amount of food available in a region also affects the size of a litter, or if there will be one at all.

A wolf's den is used only for raising pups. The den is usually located on high ground near water, with loose dirt marking the entrance. Gray wolves do not use nesting materials. They dig deep tunnels, sometimes several, leading into a maternity den. Arctic wolves, however, must survive where the ground remains frozen year round. They use a den in a cave or rock cleft (an opening caused by a split) instead. Mexican wolves prefer to live in high country. Their dens are found mostly in oak woodlands.

A pair of arctic wolves travels together during the early spring.

Half Dog/Half Wolf

Pets that are half gray wolf and half dog became popular in the United States during the early 1990s. People intentionally bred wolves with such dogs as Alaskan malamutes, Siberian huskies, and German shepherds. Though the results were unique, the cross-bred animals proved to be unreliable pets. Many were known to display wolf-like behavior—even attacking their owners and others. These animals were brought to shelters, where they were ultimately destroyed. Such trial breedings of

wild animals with domestic species proved to be failures, especially for the offspring. But this experience was a valuable lesson. It showed many people that wild animals have instincts that are very different from those of household pets. It is not fair to a wolf or a pet owner to put a partially wild animal in a domesticated setting and expect it to behave like a companion animal. It is far better to respect and appreciate wild animals in their natural settings, where they are meant to be.

Wolf Pups

Wolf pups are born blind, deaf, and helpless. The young are completely dependent on their mothers. Mothers lick their newborns to clean them, give comfort, and create a bond through scent. Being licked encourages pups to breathe, urinate, and defecate (make a bowel movement). Pups begin to play near the den at about 3 weeks of age. A guardian, not necessarily a parent, is always nearby to watch and protect the new family members.

These gray wolf pups are nearly 9 weeks old, and have recently moved out of their den.

The rough-and-tumble play of wolf pups establishes an order of dominance within the litter. Later, it helps them to bond with each other, creating a communal spirit that firmly binds the pack.

Pups begin to eat meat at about 4 weeks. The adults in the pack first provide re-gurgitated (partially digested) meat. When adults return from the hunt, the pups jump up and bite the muzzles and throats of the adults. This stimulates the regurgitation. At 2 months, the pups are moved from the maternity den to a group meeting place. By the end of the first summer, the youngsters are able to go on pack hunts. Some pups leave the pack when they reach 1 year old, others stay longer. A wolf seldom lives more than 9 years.

Top: A young gray wolf pup gets an introduction to prey.
Middle: A pup wanders out of its den.
Bottom: Biting the muzzle of an adult stimulates the feeding process.

Wolves and Humans

Humans are a wolf's only serious predator. Many wolves are threatened by human activities—even in national parks, where they are supposedly protected. Arctic wolves still roam their original range, probably because they seldom encounter people. It is the only subspecies of gray wolf that is unharmed by humans.

A wolf's most serious natural enemies are humans. Only respect and concern for the wolf's natural habitat will ensure its survival.

In Minnesota, there are about 2,200 eastern timber wolves left. They are still classified as a threatened species, but people are requesting permission to hunt them. Property owners want to shoot wolves that supposedly attack livestock or pets.

Despite misleading rumors and exaggerations about the fierceness of wolves, there have only been 3 documented attacks by wolves on humans in North America—none fatal. Protecting wolves from humans is difficult. A wolf's best protection from extinction is its instinctive shyness. But this alone cannot save the species. Humans must do their part to ensure that wolves and their habitats remain unharmed. Only then will some of nature's most fascinating survival specialists continue to play their part in the never-ending cycle of life.

Gray Wolf Facts

Scientific Name: *Canis lupus*

Shoulder Height: 26" to 38" (66 to 76 cm)

Body Length: 35" to 59" (90 to 150 cm)

Tail Length: 14" to 20" (35 to 50 cm)

Weight: 50 to 175 pounds (23 to 80 kg)

Color: Dusky gray, black, white, or silver

Reaches Sexual Maturity: 2 years

Gestation: 63 days

Litter Born: 1 per year

Litter Size: 1 to 12 pups (depends on availability of food)

Social Life: Highly structured in each pack

Favorite Food: Deer, moose, caribou

Range: Throughout Alaska and Canada; Northern Minnesota, Wisconsin, Michigan, Wyoming, Idaho, Washington, and southern Arizona

Glossary

ambush To hide and then attack.
dominance Most powerful; in control.
endurance Able to last for a long time.
gorge Eat more than necessary.
pitch The high or low end of a noise.
plaintive Sad and mournful.
regurgitate To bring back from stomach to mouth.

stalk To hunt or track in a quiet, secret way; usually following prey.
submission Following someone else's orders or lead.
tundra An area where the deeper soil is permanently frozen.

For More Information

Books

Dahl, Michael. *Wolf.* Danbury, CT: Children's Press, 1997.

Ling, Mary. Jerry Young (Photographer). *Amazing Wolves, Dogs & Foxes* (Eyewitness Juniors). New York, NY: Knopf, 1991.

Swinburne, Stephen R. Jim Brandenburg. *Once a Wolf: How Wildlife Biologist Brought Back the Gray Wolf.* Boston, MA: Houghton Mifflin, 1999.

Web Site

International Wolf Center
Information on Yellowstone wolves—www.wolf.org.

Index